Spiritual Maturity
Based on
Qualifications for Biblical Elders

An evaluation designed to help determine a person's
Christian maturity, measured by the standards set forth in:

Titus 1:6-9, 1 Timothy 3:2-7, 1 Peter 5:1-4, Acts 20:28

Christian Maturity: Based on the Qualifications for Biblical Elders

Published by:

Biblical Eldership Resources

c/o Lewis and Roth Publishers

307 Delaware Dr.

Colorado Springs, CO 80909

phone: (800) 477-3239

email: biblicaleldership@gmail.com

website: www.BiblicalEldership.com

Second Edition 2018

Copyright © 2018 Biblical Eldership Resources

Acknowledgments

This study is a joint effort of the Biblical Eldership Resources team. But we acknowledge the input from many elders who through many interactions have unknowingly affected our understanding of these qualifications and help us to see them as not being limited to leaders of the church, but as characteristics to which all Christians should aspire.

We first discovered the idea of a qualifications test from John Hopler and the Great Commission Churches Organization. We have taken the idea and expanded on it for a more robust study. But we appreciate their work in this area.

We want to dedicate this book to the elders of local churches around the world, those who "shepherd the flock of God among you," day in and day out. Their faithful and sacrificial efforts in service of the Chief Shepherd will be duly rewarded with the crown of life when he returns (1 Pet 5:2, 4). While many others may benefit from this study about elder qualifications, it is elders and potential elders who were on our radar screens as we wrote this book. In a day and age when popular preachers and writers are given much prominence in the Christian community, local church elders are the real spiritual heroes, though unsung and unheralded.

May the Lord help elders, as a result of this study, grow in their character and in their ability to shepherd the people of God. And we pray also that this blessing would extend to those who look over the shoulders of elders to embrace this study in their own pursuit of spiritual maturity.

The BER Team

INTRODUCTION

This book represents a study of the qualifications for elders of a local church as outlined in the New Testament. The target readership is elders and potential elders. However, as many have recognized, all of these qualifications are listed elsewhere in Scripture as standards for Christian maturity. What makes these unique for elders is that they are collected in two primary lists in Scripture targeted for elders, along with a few other passages. In essence, the qualifications represent the standard of spiritual maturity that all Christians should strive to attain. Anyone wanting to grow spiritually would be well-served to study the picture of maturity found in the elder qualifications.

Getting the Most out of This Study »

Christian growth comes through reading and thinking, and also by applying and embracing. To help you get the most benefit from this study we have presented below one lesson for each of the elder qualifications. These are grouped into six different categories. For each qualification, we give a notation of the Scripture(s) where it is found, a brief summary, a full description, related verses where the quality is applied to all Christians, and finally, four test or "measurement" questions (which we will explain below) to help you measure how you are doing in that area of Christian maturity.

You can skip ahead and begin the study, but to get the most out of it, we recommend continuing with some background issues that will help put the qualifications into context and with suggestions for effective use of this material.

Some Difficulties »

The wording of the qualifications may vary in different published lists, particularly as the various English translations don't always render the underlying Greek words consistently. This occurs not only between the different Bible versions, but at times also within a single translation. We have attempted to sort this out, recognizing that the meanings overlap at times as the translators wrestle with the precise rendering. In some cases, we have resorted to the original Greek for consistency, which may not match with some of the English translations. This is more of a technical issue that shouldn't cause problems for the average Christian but may be noticeable for those concerned with details. We have predominantly used the New American Standard translation, and noted when other translations are used.

CHRISTIAN GROWTH COMES THROUGH READING AND THINKING, AND ALSO BY APPLYING AND EMBRACING.

For All Christians »

While these lists, properly speaking, are targeted at elders, all of these qualifications can be seen elsewhere in Scripture as describing the goal of maturity for all Christians. All Christians should be striving for these qualities, though elders in particular should be farther down the path of maturity than the others in the congregation. Thus, we see in these lists a great standard for all Christians.

In the descriptions of the elder qualifications later in this book, we have included Scripture passages that show, either directly or indirectly, that all Christians should strive for these qualities. Some connections are obvious—for example, an elder should be hospitable (1 Tim 3:2), but all Christians likewise should be hospitable as an outworking of a committed, sacrificial lifestyle (Rom 12:1-2,13). Other connections are more parallel—for example, an elder must be Spirit-appointed to the work of an elder (Acts 20:28), but each and every Christian likewise is Spirit-appointed and has a Spirit-given gift that he or she should exercise (1 Cor 12:7-11). While the elders are to be "able to teach" (1 Tim 3:1), all Christians, if they are mature, should advance past the spiritual infancy stage to the point where they "ought to be teachers" (Heb 5:12).

As men strive to embody the qualifications listed for elders, they provide a living example of what godliness looks like in human form. In other words, elders lead the congregation toward Christian maturity by their modeling genuine Christian character. They lead by being out in front in the quest for spiritual growth.

It is our prayer that all Christians will benefit from this study, joining those whom God has raised up to be elders, following their lead toward spiritual maturity.

....

Potential and Existing Elders

We recommend that a potential elder study this material with his wife, and that both he and she answer the four questions on each page in order to identify how well he measures up to each qualification. Also, an existing elder, along with one other key leader in the church who knows the potential elder well, should evaluate him based on the four questions for each qualification.

....

Men Who Want to Prepare for One Day Becoming Elder

Knowing that we humans tend toward self-deception, we highly recommend having others study this material with you and to have them evaluate you. This can be done in a mentoring situation, in an accountability partnership or as husband and wife. The goal is to help you to 1) be encouraged where you can identify spiritual growth in your life, and 2) uncover areas where growth is needed, things that you may not presently be aware of. This becomes a useful tool for helping fulfill what Scripture says: "Iron sharpens iron, so one man sharpens another" (Pr 27:17).

> THEY PROVIDE A LIVING EXAMPLE OF WHAT GODLINESS LOOKS LIKE IN HUMAN FORM.

How Many Qualifications Are There? »

The published lists tend to differ in length, combining various qualifications where there are similarities. We have used a maximal approach, trying to capture the nuanced differences where that would be helpful. But the length of our list also reflects the fact that we have included in our study not only 1 Timothy 3 and Titus 1, but also 1 Peter 5 and Acts 20. In all, we count thirty-one qualifications.

How Perfectly Should a Person Measure Up? »

Of course, anyone who honestly and humbly studies the qualifications for being an elder recognizes that no one will ever measure up fully. However, lest we justify poorly qualified elders, the question is begged, "Is there a minimum compliance required?" Answering this question is somewhat of an exercise of subjectivity, but nonetheless it must be considered. While some qualifications are easier to judge than others (for example, a man who has had an affair is clearly disqualified), others are not so easy (to what degree must children show evidence of obedience?). However, despite the relative nature of these qualifications, there are clearly some things that can be said about them.

The level of maturity for a newer church (where most everyone is relatively new to faith) may not be as stringent as that for an established church (where the level of maturity is much greater). After all, if the new church has to wait for "very mature" leadership, it may have to wait too long, thus establishing unrecoverable dependency on the church planter or missionary. This, in fact, is not uncommon on the mission field. The better part of wisdom suggests that elders generally be farther along the road to maturity, as measured by the elder qualifications, than those whom they will be shepherding.

A too-stringent compliance requirement may disqualify every potential shepherd. On the other hand, taking these qualifications too loosely can hinder the work of the Spirit greatly. Many established churches have been ruined by men of questionable character holding unrelentingly to the office of elder. Therefore, we conclude the qualification should be used as a measure that a man should be moving toward, and he should be farther down the road in that process of spiritual growth than the people whom he shepherds. At the same time, the church dare not accept inadequately qualified men into leadership.

Who makes the determination? Ideally, the existing elders are in the best position, being substantially qualified and maturing themselves, to identify those men who also are moving ahead in their spiritual maturation. In the case of a new congregation, it would be the church planter(s) or missionaries who are establishing the church. Of course, feedback from the congregation is important as well, for many of the qualifications have to do with a man's reputation.

THE QUALIFICATION SHOULD BE USED AS A MEASURE THAT A MAN SHOULD BE MOVING TOWARD.

Best Practices for Using This Study »

The best way to use this resource is to study each qualification, one at a time:

• Begin with prayer.

• Read through the page, looking up all the Scripture references to see them in their contexts.

• Answer the four questions at the end of each page, praying the Lord would help you assess that qualification in your life.

• Enter that total in the Measurement Chart at the end of the book.

• Determine any action steps you need to take for growing in that area.

How to Use the Measurement Questions »

The purpose of measurement questions is not to rate the spirituality or maturity of the individual but to determine how well he measures up to the qualifications—which areas he is doing well in and which areas he needs to work on. For each question, enter a numerical answer:

 No   Mostly No   Neutral   Mostly Yes   Yes

Record a "5" if a question does not apply (e.g., a question as to children if the man has no children). No blank should be left empty. Then add the four answers for a total and insert that number on the Summary Sheet at the end of this book.

In the end, the perfect individual (of which there is only the Lord Jesus Christ!) would measure a perfect score of 155. But there is no grading involved, nor scoring in comparison with others. This is simply a tool to help identify areas on which to improve.

The individual being evaluated should meet with each person evaluating him and discuss the results. Review together each qualification, particularly the ones that received a low "score." These may indicate areas for concerted effort to address in the individual's life. For each qualification that seems to be lacking, an action plan needs to be taken to promote growth in that area. This might include identifying and memorizing relevant passages, spending time in focused prayer, establishing accountability with someone to whom the individual will answer for his growth in that area of his Christian life, and reading relevant articles and books on the topic.

Remember, the goal is spiritual growth, so that you can become a model for others to follow—whether you are an elder, a potential elder, or someone who wants to be a spiritual influence through your example of godly character.

May the Lord strengthen you through the process of honestly evaluating your spiritual life, as you become a growing Christian leader or influencer for Christ.

BACKGROUNDS TO THE KEY PASSAGES

Helpful to consider are the backgrounds to each of the main passages on elder qualifications, which we will briefly address now.

....

1 Timothy 3:1-7 »

All indicators point to Paul's young protégé Timothy being stationed in Ephesus (1 Tim 1:3, compare with 2 Tim 4:12-13). And if this was the case, by the time Paul wrote this first letter to Timothy (around 63 A.D.), the church at Ephesus had been well-taught by Priscilla and Aquila and by Apollos, who was mighty in the Scriptures (Acts 18:2, 19-28). In addition, the apostle Paul himself spent over two years there teaching daily in the school of Tyrannus (Acts 19:8-10). It was reported by Luke, the chronicler of the book of Acts, that at Ephesus, "the word of the Lord was growing mightily and prevailing" (Acts 19:20). The letter Paul wrote to the church there reflects a mature audience (in contrast to, say, the carnal church in Corinthians), and the apostle deals with more advanced themes, such as the nature of the church and theologically deeper understanding of various aspects of our salvation, election, redemption, regeneration, etc.

Also, we read in the book of Acts that toward the end of Paul's third missionary tour, he spent some time with the elders from Ephesus, giving them his famous farewell speech—essential reading and memorization for anyone seeking to be a spiritual leader. So the church by that time already had identifiable elders. Therefore, we conclude that when Paul wrote his first letter to Timothy, the believers in Ephesus—where Timothy lived and labored in ministry—were well-taught and fairly mature as a church.

> **IF ANY MAN ASPIRES TO THE OFFICE OF OVERSEER, IT IS A FINE WORK HE DESIRES TO DO.**

Now in this letter to Timothy, notice Paul's initial reference in the passage on qualifications concerns those who aspire to the office of overseer. "It is a trustworthy statement: if any man aspires to the office of overseer, it is a fine work he desires to do" (1 Tim 3:1). The apostle had in mind—at least initially—those who were not yet elders. But he quickly switched to the generic: "An overseer, then, must be...." In other words, if a man seeks to be an elder, this is what he aspires to, to be a man described in the following verses.

That no man can fulfill these qualifications perfectly must be assumed as a matter of course. So no man should wait until he has become perfectly qualified—spiritual maturation is an ongoing process until we enter the Lord's presence. We conclude that these "qualifications" help existing elders to gauge their own spiritual maturity, but also set the goal of maturity that potential elders should consider as well. Not a hard, cold, fast list, but when used in the hands of godly elders, it is tremendously beneficial. This is the context in which the desire to be an elder is a desire for a "fine work." It is really a desire to be the kind of man described in the qualifications that makes the work "fine" rather than an earthly power position.

It should seem obvious that the existing elders would read these things and be challenged to live up to that standard. In fact, as with all of the Christian life, elders need to keep moving forward, growing and maturing. This is the example of the apostle Paul, who wrote, "Not that I have already obtained it or have already become perfect, but I press on so that I may lay hold of that for which also I was laid hold of by Christ Jesus ... I press on toward the goal for the prize of the upward call of God in Christ Jesus" (Phil 3:12, 14).

Titus 1:5-9 »

In Paul's letter to Titus, on the other hand, he writes concerning leadership for churches that are not yet mature. He begins, "For this reason I left you in Crete, that you would set in order what remains and appoint elders in every city as I directed you..." (Tit 1:5) and then goes on to list elder character traits. The phrase "what remains" is rendered from a single Greek word *leipo*, which means "that which falls short or is lacking." Paul did not use this word in writing to Timothy, where the church was fully established and complete with elders already in place. The churches in Crete, in contrast, were apparently new gatherings of believers with no leadership structure in place—and that is what was lacking. Without elders, Paul considered the churches to be in disorder, incomplete.

So in the context of Paul's letter to Titus, the list of qualifications can more readily be seen as a list of requirements to identify potential elders in the fledgling churches of Crete, or a list of traits men must be moving toward if they are considering the work of being an elder or leader in the church.

In light of the contextual differences between Paul's two letters, some have attempted to explain why Timothy's list seems more comprehensive than Titus' list. There may be merit to such analysis, but we resist such conjectures and take both lists together as a whole to indicate God's desire for the spiritual leadership of the church, for both potential and existing elders.

Acts 20:17-38 »

While not including a list of elder qualifications (in comparison with 1 Timothy 3 and Titus 1), Paul's farewell speech to the Ephesian elders is the most comprehensive teaching specifically directed to elders in Scripture, in terms of what elders do. In this message, Paul presents himself as a model of spiritual leadership—a trait all elders should possess—namely, being an example or model for others to follow. Peter affirmed this trait of modeling in his instruction to the elders among scattered Christians throughout the northeastern Mediterranean area (1 Pet 5:3).

Here, Paul added to the overall list of qualifications one important requirement: that elders are Spirit-appointed (Acts 20:28). "Be on guard for yourselves and for all the flock, among which the Holy Spirit has made you overseers..." (Acts 20:28). Without the Spirit's appointment, nothing else matters, and so we include this in our study as a necessary qualification for elders.

1 Peter 5:1-4 »

The apostle Peter wrote to elders who lived among the scattered, persecuted believers in and around Galatia and Asia around 60-62 A.D. In the context of their difficulties, he exhorted them with a brief passage to shepherd the flock of God with the right motives and not for ulterior reasons. The unique perspective he brings to this question of elder qualifications is that even in times of persecution and hardship, elders should be men of good character and right motives.

CONTENTS   Elder Qualifications

SPIRIT-MOTIVATED Desire

Summary:
First and foremost, a man becomes an elder through appointment by the Spirit of God, not because he decides to be an elder. That is his primary motivation.

Key Verse:
"Be on guard for yourselves and for all the flock, among which the Holy Spirit has made you overseers, to shepherd the church of God which He purchased with His own blood." **(Acts 20:28)**

Description »

First and foremost, the overriding qualification for being an elder is that a man must be Holy Spirit-appointed. Just like the Spirit "set apart" and "sent out" Barnabas and Paul (Acts 13:3-3) as the first missionaries, God sets apart men as elders for the wonderfully important task of shepherding God's people. The rest of the biblical qualifications are best seen as the criteria for recognizing whom the Lord raises up. He is the one who places men into this service, and rightly so—for it is His church which "He purchased with His own blood." He paid dearly for the redemption of souls, and the shepherd can be nothing less than Spirit-selected.

Elders must have a keen sense and conviction that they serve at the Lord's pleasure, by His choice. This provides the primary motivation to first of all do the work of shepherding, and also to do it well, as befitting a blood-bought community whom God considers eternally valuable. It is not sufficient for an elder to feel compelled by the need, or because he was asked, or because there is some quorum to fill. Nor does it mean that a seminary education is sufficient to be an elder. And it does not mean that an elder remains an elder for life, for the Lord may remove a man's "set apartness" to the work. The Spirit is the one who decides. »

And it means that elders do not primarily serve people, they serve the Lord—to please Him, not to please the people. And because they serve the Lord, they care for those whom the Lord cares for—namely His people. In other words, they serve and care for the people of God because they serve the God who cares for them.

Applied to All Christians »

"Now there are varieties of gifts, but the same Spirit. And there are varieties of ministries, and the same Lord. There are varieties of effects, but the same God who works all things in all persons. But to each one is given the manifestation of the Spirit for the common good." **(1 Corinthians 12:4-7)**

Questions » (1-No, 2-Mostly No, 3-Neutral, 4-Mostly Yes, 5-Yes)

1. Do you have a genuine sense that the Holy Spirit is calling you to be a shepherd of God's people?	
2. Is your desire confirmed by the Spirit through the counsel of godly people in your life?	
3. Do you have circumstantial evidence that the Holy Spirit has used you in shepherding others?	
4. Have you had a history of recognizing the Spirit's confirmation of serving in other areas?	
Enter the total here and on the "Measurement Chart" (page 74)	

GODLY DESIRE | 🔥Desire

Summary:
An elder must have a godly desire to do the work of overseeing the church, not just the position.

Key Verse:
"It is a trustworthy statement: if any man aspires to the office of overseer, it is a fine work he desires to do."
(1 Timothy 3:1)

Description »

Scripture places a premium on men who desire to do the work of an elder, by leading off the list of qualifications with this "trustworthy statement" (code-speak for emphasizing importance—see also 1 Tim 1:15, 4:9; 2 Tim 2:11). But what drives this desire to be an elder? It should not be personal ambition for power or honor; the desire must be grounded in the prior appointment by the Holy Spirit (Acts 20:28).

Notice the focus of this desire is not on an office or position so much as it is the work of being an elder. The context makes things clear with the last phrase, "it is a fine work he desires." While it is human nature to strive for positions of power and honor, church leaders should have a godly desire not for the position, but for doing the actual serving as a spiritual leader. He does not serve for his own benefit—"not for sordid gain...nor yet as lording it over ..." (1 Pet 5:2).

This desire, though, is more than a superficial willingness to serve in one of many options. To "aspire" means to "stretch out to or reach after." The man Paul envisions has a driving passion to shepherd the people of God. And the actual work is described as "overseer," one who watches over with a keen eye like a shepherd watches over his flock, ready to act in whatever way is best for them.

We can conclude that this role of "overseeing" is a work of the elders because of the close association between the words » "overseers" and "elders" in Paul's letters (see 1 Tim 5:17; 19; Tit 1:5, 7). "Overseer" (*episcopos* in Greek) emphasizes the function, while "elder" emphasizes the maturity.

If a man is Spirit-appointed and has a godly desire to shepherd God's people, then it follows that he must aspire to the qualifications or character traits Paul lists out in 1 Timothy 3:2-7.

....

Applied to All Christians »

"But earnestly desire the greater gifts..."
(1 Corinthians 12:31)

"Pursue love, yet desire earnestly spiritual gifts..."
(1 Corinthians 14:1)

....

Questions » (**1**-No, **2**-Mostly No, **3**-Neutral, **4**-Mostly Yes, **5**-Yes)

1. Does your desire for being an elder reflect a godly motivation to shepherd, rather than a desire to advance yourself?	
2. Do you choose to focus on serving God's people above your own hobbies?	
3. Do you see value in caring for people spiritually, apart from being an elder?	
4. Would you willingly submit, without bitterness or anger, if it was decided that you should not become an elder at this time?	
Enter the total here and on the "Measurement Chart" (page 74)	

EAGER TO SERVE | Desire

Summary:
An elder is one who serves as an eager, willing volunteer (whether financially supported or not), for he is motivated by the return of the Chief Shepherd.

Key Verse:
"Shepherd the flock of God among you, exercising oversight... with eagerness..."
(1 Peter 5:2)

Description »

Clearly, God's desire is for the church to be led by willing, eager elders, not reluctant ones. The work, when done with a shepherd's heart and with godly motivation, can be very difficult. Many elders strain under the burden. The man who desires power and honor will soon wilt, stagnate, or become derailed in this good work—and the people will suffer. What makes elders stand out is a "willingness to sacrifice." One does not serve as a shepherd of God's people with money as his primary motivation. A shepherd will shepherd whether or not there is financial remuneration. The "financial support," if there is any, does not provide motivation, but provides time, so the elder can spend fewer hours earning his wages and more time being about the work of shepherding.

If a person is resistant to shepherding God's people without pay, then pay will not motivate him to godly shepherding. This "voluntariness" must be accompanied by eagerness, enthusiasm, and cheerfulness. A person may be willing to volunteer as an elder, but to do it with joy is a sign of the true shepherd's heart.

So what motivates the elder to be willing and eager while carrying the burden of shepherding? The answer is that "when the Chief Shepherd appears, you will receive the unfading crown of glory" (1 Pet 5:4).

Applied to All Christians »

"If I then, the Lord and the Teacher, washed your feet, you also ought to wash one another's feet. For I gave you an example that you also should do as I did to you." (John 13:14–15)

Questions » (1-No, 2-Mostly No, 3-Neutral, 4-Mostly Yes, 5-Yes)

1. Do you show enthusiasm for serving in the church, even in the physical areas?	
2. Are you the kind of person to help out readily when asked or where there is an obvious need?	
3. Do you spontaneously show spiritual interest in people during fellowship times and before and after church meetings?	
4. Do you willingly take on responsibility?	
Enter the total here and on the "Measurement Chart" (page 74)	

NOT RELUCTANT ⑥ Desire

Summary:
A man must not serve out of compulsion but in submission to the Spirit.

Key Verse:
"Shepherd the flock of God among you, exercising oversight, not under compulsion..." **(1 Peter 5:2)**

Description »

While Paul says that he was "obligated" to preach the gospel (Rom 1:14), and we are obligated to "not live according to the flesh," nowhere are individuals told that they are "obligated" to serve as elders. The idea is not to be men who serve out of necessity or constraint, or as one writer put it, being compelled "in a manner that cannot be evaded." Men who serve under compulsion, whatever the source, should not be elders—if that is their primary reason for serving.

There are many reasons why a person might serve as an elder out of obligation or compulsion: 1) expectations from others, including one's wife; 2) a pressing need for more leaders; 3) an inner sense of inferiority and need to "achieve," making one feel obligated to fulfill personal needs in ungodly ways; and 4) the pressing needs of the congregation. In most congregations, it would be safe to say, there are not enough godly leaders willing to make the personal sacrifice to shoulder the burden of watching over the people of God and meeting their spiritual needs. Yet, despite our sense of urgency, we must never compel men to be elders, nor allow others to compel us to serve as elders.

The man who is feeling compelled by the Holy Spirit finds his motivation falling in line with the Spirit, and this will be reflected in a willing eagerness. But a man must see beyond the human coercions so that he won't be blinded to the Spirit's leading. And the existing elders must allow the Spirit to motivate those whom He desires, lest we find unqualified, unwilling men serving as defective shepherds of God's people.

Applied to All Christians »

"As each one has received a special gift, employ it in serving one another as good stewards of the manifold grace of God. Whoever speaks is to do so as one who is speaking the utterances of God; whoever serves is to do so as one who is serving by the strength which God supplies; so that in all things God may be glorified through Jesus Christ, to whom belongs the glory and dominion forever and ever. Amen." **(1 Peter 4:10–11)**

Questions » (**1**-No, **2**-Mostly No, **3**-Neutral, **4**-Mostly Yes, **5**-Yes)

1. Do you desire to be an elder without any foreboding, obsessive sense of heaviness?	
2. Does your wife lovingly encourage you to become an elder, without pressuring you?	
3. Do you genuinely desire to do the work of an elder without feeling that there is no alternative because the church needs leaders?	
4. Have you dealt with all the hesitations of inadequacies, uncertainties, or doubts about being an elder?	
Enter the total here and on the "Measurement Chart" (page 74)	

ABOVE REPROACH |  Integrity

Summary:
"Above reproach" is the umbrella word over every other qualification. It refers to the public and private character and quality of the elder's life.

Key Verses:
"An overseer, then, must be above reproach..."
(1 Timothy 3:2)

"For the overseer must be above reproach as God's steward..." (Titus 1:7)

Description »

If we could summarize the qualifications for elders in two words, we would say "above reproach." In 1 Timothy 3:2, the underlying word can be translated "without stain," and in Titus 1:7 it can be translated "blameless." This qualification is the umbrella word that encompasses most all the other qualifications. In fact, in 1 Timothy 3:2 it forms a bookend for the qualifications list with 1 Timothy 1:7, where we find an elder must have a "good reputation."

All the qualifications that come after "above reproach" are examples of being "above reproach." This means the elder's life does not give fuel for personal attack or criticism. While he is not perfect, he should be blameless—that is, any accusations or challenges to his integrity will not hold up when fully examined.

This qualification is best understood in its context. It can be easily understood by the positive and negative examples Paul lists. For example, a man who is not faithful to his spouse is not above reproach. A man who is not sober-minded is not above reproach. A man who is not respectable is not above reproach, etc.

Positively, an elder should be a hospitable man, a good manager of his family, etc. So while there is a public and a private aspect to this qualification, that is being without stain and blameless, Paul does not seem to be arguing for some kind of sinless » perfection. He is saying that his character, whether observable or private, is that of integrity.

So in one sense, this first qualification that the apostle gives is the most generic and the most important. It's the "catch-all" qualification, the umbrella that covers every other qualification that the apostle lists. Everything about the elders should be above reproach to the observation of those he shepherds.

......

Applied to All Christians »

"...prove yourselves to be blameless and innocent, children of God above reproach in the midst of a crooked and perverse generation, among whom you appear as lights in the world..."

(Philippians 2:15)

"Prescribe these things as well, so that they may be above reproach." **(1 Timothy 5:7)**

......

Questions » (1-No, 2-Mostly No, 3-Neutral, 4-Mostly Yes, 5-Yes)

1. Is it true that no one has an unresolved, justifiable complaint against you?	
2. Do those closest to you (wife, relatives, friends) believe you are qualified to be an elder?	
3. Do you have any unconfessed sins or negative traits that are obvious to others?	
4. Are you open and vulnerable to accept constructive criticism about your personal life?	
Enter the total here and on the "Measurement Chart" (page 74)	

GOOD REPUTATION |  Integrity

Summary:
The elder must have a good reputation with those outside the Church; otherwise he will bring shame on himself and the Church, falling into the trap of Satan.

Key Verse:
"And he must have a good reputation with those outside the church, so that he will not fall into reproach and the snare of the devil." **(1 Timothy 3:7)**

Description »

This qualification reminds us that there is a public aspect to eldership. The Lord and His Church are not only concerned with the private aspects of the leader's life; they are also concerned with the visible perception of his behavior. The name and character of our Savior and His body are at stake. If an elder is excellent in the assembly and among believers, but is crooked in his business, a poor neighbor, or an embarrassing member of his extended family, then he is disqualified from the office. Together, the inner life of a person, his behavior among believers, and his reputation among non-believers all make up the character of an elder.

When a shepherd of God's people (who is to model Christ-likeness) fails in his public reputation among non-believers, his hypocrisy has the greater effect of bringing disgrace on the church and those in the church. Satan will leap on this opportunity to handicap and neutralize the spiritual power of the elder and bring shame on the whole church (see Rev 12:10, "the accuser of the brethren"). Is not hypocrisy one of the chief criticisms the world has of those claiming to be Christ-followers? This qualification will guard the elders, the leaders of God's people, from this criticism.

The elder's character must therefore be demonstrated and proven in the church and in the world. Not only is the world » watching for failure by church leaders; so is Satan. But if the man is well thought of by outsiders and has a positive reputation in the community, then the Lord and His Church will be glorified and magnified, and there will be less ammunition with which Satan or non-believers can accuse the Church.

Applied to All Christians »

"Keep your behavior excellent among the Gentiles, so that in the thing in which they slander you as evildoers, they may because of your good deeds, as they observe them, glorify God in the day of visitation." (1 Peter 2:12, see Romans 5:4)

Questions » (1-No, 2-Mostly No, 3-Neutral, 4-Mostly Yes, 5-Yes)

1. Do fellow employees and workers who are unbelievers appreciate and value you?	
2. Are you honest, demonstrating integrity in business and personal dealings?	
3. Is your social life a good testimony before non-Christians?	
4. Do your neighbors respect you?	
Enter the total here and on the "Measurement Chart" (page 74)	

RESPECTABLE |  Integrity

Summary:
The elder must be an orderly, well-behaved man, enjoying respect from most people.

Key Verse:
An overseer must be "...respectable..." **(1 Timothy 3:2)**

Description »

The beauty of God's work is that He transforms things from chaos (disorder) to order (cosmos). We see this transformation in the creation account in Genesis 1:1-2:3. The earth started "without form and void," but God brings order to chaos, and we end up with Adam and Eve in a beautiful garden, filled with good things (and one prohibited thing). We also see it in the New Testament when our Lord was accosted by Legion, a man possessed and tormented by many demons. This man was a disaster to himself and to his community. When Jesus freed him from demonic domination, he became a new man. Here was a man who once raged among the tombs, inflicting harm to himself and anyone whom he encountered. He terrorized his region. But when he met Jesus and was delivered from demonic dominion, we find him "sitting down, clothed, and in his right mind" (Mark 5:15).

It is this orderliness, this "having it all together," that should characterize the elder. Most translations render it "respectable," but the sense is that of having one's life in right order. This should be something that is both external and internal. Outward appearances should reflect the inward order that characterizes the elder. To be merely external would be hypocrisy. To be merely internal would be insufficient. In contrast to those whose lives are in chaos, the elder's life reflects the cosmos, which is the result of God's transforming work through Christ and His Spirit. »

Interestingly, the related word is used in 1 Timothy 2:9 to describe a godly woman's clothing as "respectable," and it may refer to a life that is not disheveled, or disorderly, in appearance.

Some people, by virtue of their well-ordered (*cosmeo*) lives, convey a dignity and presence that is evident and prompts respect.

....

Applied to All Christians »

"Likewise, I want women to adorn themselves with proper [ESV: respectable] clothing, modestly and discreetly, not with braided hair and gold or pearls or costly garments..."
(1 Timothy 2:9)

....

Questions » (**1**-No, **2**-Mostly No, **3**-Neutral, **4**-Mostly Yes, **5**-Yes)

1. Do you generally seem to be a person who "has it all together"— your life seems well-ordered?	
2. Does your external appearance measure up to what is considered proper both biblically and culturally?	
3. Do you regularly plan out your time?	
4. Do you keep your priorities?	
Enter the total here and on the "Measurement Chart" (page 74)	

DEVOUT | ⊘ Integrity

Summary:
Holiness must be both experienced by and evidenced in the life of every church leader.

Key Verse:
The overseer must be "...devout..." **(Titus 1:8)**

Description »

The qualifying requirement to be devout demands that elders move beyond the positional holiness granted by God. It confronts them with the requirement to show evidence of the practice of holiness in their lives. The injunction here is therefore not only that the church leader be a child of God, but that his life reflect the characteristics of godly holiness.

What does that mean? The expectation is that the life of the elder should be "undefiled by sin, free from wickedness, pure, holy, pious" (Strong's, G3741). The focus is on living. This requires an intentional response; it's a demand to show evidence of the work of Christ in the person. It takes discipline, a striving to live daily by seeking its example in Christ Jesus.

The Bible calls Jesus the Holy One in Acts 2:27. He became High Priest, holy, harmless, undefiled and separate from sinners (Heb 7:26). He both was holy and displayed holiness. The life of Jesus is therefore every Christian's gold standard. Christ's perfect life makes for a perfect example. In fact, we are to be looking at Jesus, the author and finisher of our faith (Heb 12:2).

The connection between holiness and holy living is clear for all Christians, especially for an elder. In setting an expectation and providing an example of holiness, the Bible removes every excuse for an elder to be otherwise. Because of this, the Bible encourages the flock in the local church to "imitate their church leaders' manner of life" (Heb 13:7).

That's modeling. The life of Christ imitated by an elder will be a good role model for others to imitate. Anything less will be a disaster.

Applied to All Christians »

"You are witnesses, and so is God, how devoutly and uprightly and blamelessly we behaved toward you believers..." **(1 Thessalonians 2:10)**

"Pure and undefiled religion in the sight of our God and Father is this: to visit orphans and widows in their distress, and to keep oneself unstained by the world." **(James 1:27)**

Questions » (**1**-No, **2**-Mostly No, **3**-Neutral, **4**-Mostly Yes, **5**-Yes)

1. Do you desire to please God more than men?	
2. Do you have a strong prayer life?	
3. Are you committed to obeying God and His Word regardless of the pressures or trials you go through?	
4. Do you acknowledge the value of other people's examples in your life?	
Enter the total here and on the "Measurement Chart" (page 74)	

UPRIGHT | 🎖 Integrity

Summary:
An elder must, by his manner of life and conduct, manifest the fruits of justification and sanctification. His piety should be evident in his conformity to the truth.

Key Verse:
The elder must be "...just..." **(Titus 1:8)**

Description »

The term "just" can be translated "upright" (NIV). The underlying adjective (*dikaios*), used very commonly in the (Greek) OT and in the NT, is closely related to the noun meaning "righteousness." In the NT our term is particularly used to describe or refer to believers who, through faith in Christ, have been declared righteous, and who therefore live uprightly, within the lines prescribed by God's Word.

This term is rendered "righteous" when used of God the Father (Ps 145:17) or the Son (Matt 27:19; Acts 3:14). When used of men, it may refer to one's conduct in conformity to the requirements of the Law (see 1 Tim 1:9; Rom 8:4).

It is possible, however, for one to outwardly appear to conform to godly standards but not actually be born of God. Such was the case with the scribes and Pharisees, who outwardly appeared to be righteous but inwardly were not (Matt 9:11-13, 23:27-28). While it is possible for a person to appear to be righteous, but fail to be truly pious or devout, it is not possible for one to be truly devout without also being upright. This may help to explain why the term *dikaios* (upright or just) is sometimes paired with the term *hosios* (holy or devout). Such is the case in Titus 1:8.

The elder, then, must not only be a believer (1 Tim 3:6; Tit 1:8-9); he must also manifest the fruit of his justification and ongoing sanctification by righteous living in his relationship to others (James 2:14; 1 John 4:20-21). When an elder is both upright and devout, he manifests the very character of God (John 17:25; Rev 16:5) and also follows the example of Paul (1 Thess 2:10).

Applied to All Christians »

"You are witnesses, and so is God, how devoutly and uprightly and blamelessly we behaved toward you believers..." **(1 Thessalonians 2:10)**

"Brethren, join in following my example, and observe those who walk according to the pattern you have in us." **(Philippians 3:17)**

Questions » (**1**-No, **2**-Mostly No, **3**-Neutral, **4**-Mostly Yes, **5**-Yes)

1. Are you fair and honest in your relationships with other people?	
2. Do you listen to both sides of a discussion before coming to a conclusion?	
3. Do others seek you out as a fair counselor?	
4. Could you confidently and righteously lead in putting out of the church someone who deserved to be removed from fellowship?	
Enter the total here and on the "Measurement Chart" (page 74)	

AN EXAMPLE | ♔ Integrity

Summary:
An elder must live his life consciously as an example to the people under his care.

Key Verse:
Shepherd the flock of God "...proving to be examples to the flock." **(1 Peter 5:3)**

Description »

"Like people, like priest," Hosea said (Hos 4:9). The self-evident connection between the strength of leadership and the character of its flock is true in churches today. Our Lord reminds us, "A pupil ... after he has been fully trained will be like his teacher" (Luke 6:40). Thus, Peter mandates the value of "proving to be examples to the flock" (1 Pet 5:3).

Paul agrees with Peter by providing himself as a model. He writes to the Corinthians, "Be imitators of me, just as I also am of Christ" (1 Cor 11:1). To the Philippians he instructs, "The things you have learned and received and heard and seen in me, practice these things..." (Phil 4:9). And to the Ephesian elders he testifies, "You yourselves know, from the first day that I set foot in Asia, how I was with you the whole time..." (Acts 20:18).

Thus, if we are to follow Paul's example, every elder should put himself out to his congregation as a model to follow. Paul writes to his young co-worker, "...be an example to the believers" (1 Tim 4:12). That is a tremendous responsibility on the elders. As Cotton Mather, the Puritan preacher, would say, "It's an office which every angel in heaven might covet to be employed in for a thousand years to come."

This principle is made to work both ways. We read that the writer of Hebrews puts a threefold charge on his readers: remember your leaders, reflect on their conduct, and imitate them (Heb 13:7). God has set a high standard for church leadership. Now go live it.

Applied to All Christians »

"...so that you became an example to all the believers in Macedonia and in Achaia."
(1 Thessalonians 1:7)

"Let no one look down on your youthfulness, but rather in speech, conduct, love, faith and purity, show yourself an example of those who believe."
(1 Timothy 4:12)

Questions » (**1**-No, **2**-Mostly No, **3**-Neutral, **4**-Mostly Yes, **5**-Yes)

1. Do others look to you as an example of Christian faith and maturity?	
2. Do you behave consciously in ways that others can imitate?	
3. Is there evidence of others modeling certain aspects of their Christian lives after your example?	
4. Do you have the desire to personally disciple others, and have you done it?	
Enter the total here and on the "Measurement Chart" (page 74)	

GOD HAS SET A HIGH STANDARD FOR CHURCH LEADERSHIP. NOW GO LIVE IT.

FAITHFUL TO THE WORD | ■ Word

Summary:
Elders must be firm in conviction of the Word of God, faithful in communicating it, and fearless in correcting those who stray from it.

Key Verse:
Appoint elders "...if any man is... holding fast the faithful word which is in accordance with the teaching, so that he will be able both to exhort in sound doctrine and to refute those who contradict."
(Titus 1:9)

Description »

As a good shepherd leads his flock to the finest grass (Ps 23:2), so elders should provide the finest spiritual food for the flock, namely God's Word. The Scripture is "life-giving" (Rom 4:17), "solid food" (Heb 5:14), "spiritual milk" (1 Pet 2:2), and "health" (Pr 4:22). It needs no additives (Pr 30:6) and no enrichment (1 Pet 2:2).

Six overriding principles can frame this elder qualification:

1. The elder, as a shepherd of God's people, must himself be firm in his conviction of the Word of God. He should not be feeble or unsure of what he believes. He is to "do [his] best to present [him]self to God as one approved, a worker who has no need to be ashamed, rightly handling the word of truth" (2 Tim 2:15).

2. Elders must provide the whole counsel of God to the full spectrum of believers at their various stages of maturity. Paul tells the Ephesian elders that he did not hesitate to proclaim to the church the full counsel of God, that is, the whole of Scripture (Acts 20:27). This begins with new believers, who need the pure milk of the Word (1 Pet 2:2). And it extends to seasoned believers as well, who should be able to teach others (Heb 5:11-14; see also Paul teaching Timothy and Titus). »

3. The good shepherd must be faithful in "rightly handling" the Word (2 Tim 2:15). He must understand good hermeneutical principles.

4. The elder shepherd is careful to apply the Word to himself first, and then to others (1 Tim 4:6, 12-16; Tit 2:6-8; Acts 20:28).

5. The godly elder must be faithful in communicating God's Word (2 Tim 4:1-4).

6. The pastoral elder must be faithful in correcting error when there is departure from the Word (1 Tim 1:3-5; 2 Tim 2:24-26).

....

Applied to All Christians »

"Therefore, let us fear if, while a promise remains of entering His rest, any one of you may seem to have come short of it. For indeed we have had good news preached to us, just as they also; but the word they heard did not profit them, because it was not united by faith in those who heard."
(Hebrews 4:1–2)

....

Questions » (**1**-No, **2**-Mostly No, **3**-Neutral, **4**-Mostly Yes, **5**-Yes)

1. Are you united with the other church leaders on all areas of major doctrine?	
2. Do you take a stand in discussions or interactions based on the Word of God?	
3. Are you actively meditating on the Word, so that you can use it readily in your personal life and interactions with others?	
4. Is there evidence that you are under submission to the Word of God (conviction of sin, repentance, change of view as a result from being shown Scripture)?	
Enter the total here and on the "Measurement Chart" (page 74)	

ABLE TO TEACH | 📖 Word

Summary:
An elder, while not necessarily required to be a gifted teacher, must be capable of showing from the Bible Christian truths and defending right doctrine.

Key Verse:
"An overseer, then, must be ...able to teach..."
(1 Timothy 3:2)

Description »

This qualification goes hand in hand with the qualification of being faithful to the Word (Tit 1:9). The elder must not only "hold fast the faithful word" (Tit 1:9a), but he must be able to "exhort in sound doctrine and to refute those who contradict" (Tit 1:9b). To do this, he must be "able to teach" the Word. This is also true of anyone who wishes to be "the Lord's bond-servant" (2 Tim 2:24).

The term *didaktikos*, translated "able" or "apt" (as the KJV puts it), is used only twice in Scripture and only once outside of the Bible (in Philo). Because of its paucity of occurrence, we cannot be precise in its meaning, but suffice it to say that an elder must have a certain ability in "accurately handling the word of truth" (2 Tim 2:15). This means he is able to show from Scripture right teaching and understanding as the specific needs and questions arise in the normal course of shepherding. This does not necessarily mean an elder is required to have the spiritual gift of teaching (1 Cor 12:28-29; Rom 12:7), in that his primary ministry may not be pulpit teaching or any other ongoing teaching venue. Rather, he has the ability to expound the Word as the need arises, whether publicly or privately. How could he protect the flock from false teaching except through laying out the correct teaching from the Word?

A large part of the eldership as a whole is involved in teaching the Word. Some may be gifted in the systematic teaching on a Sunday morning. Others may be more suited to Sunday school classes or small groups. All should be able to expound the Scripture when called upon, and when necessary in the normal life of shepherding others.

Applied to All Christians »

"For though by this time you ought to be teachers, you have need again for someone to teach you the elementary principles of the oracles of God, and you have come to need milk and not solid food." **(Hebrews 5:12)**

Questions » (**1**-No, **2**-Mostly No, **3**-Neutral, **4**-Mostly Yes, **5**-Yes)

1. Do you enjoy reading and studying the Word in preparation to share the Word?	
2. Is there clear growth in the lives of those people with whom you share the Word?	
3. Do you freely share the Word of God in your interactions with people?	
4. Do you participate well in small group Bible studies, showing an aptitude for being able to explain Scripture?	
Enter the total here and on the "Measurement Chart" (page 74)	

Exhort In Sound Doctrine | 📖 Word

Summary:
An elder must be able and ready to proclaim and teach the core doctrines of Scripture.

Key Verse:
The overseer must be "...able both to exhort in sound doctrine and to refute those who contradict..."
(Titus 1:9)

Description »

The under-shepherd is to guard and hold fast to the faithful word (Titus 1:9a). He must be able to "exhort in sound doctrine and to refute those who contradict" (Titus 1:9b). Elders are to be men who know the Word of God and trumpet the words of God. Since the local church is "a pillar and buttress of the truth" (1 Tim. 3:15b), its leaders must be rock-solid pillars of biblical doctrine or the house will crumble.

At a minimum, an elder must firmly adhere to orthodox and historic, biblical teaching. The Lord wants elders who are laboring in teaching and preaching the Word of God. This is HIS design! They don't just sit on a board making decisions, but are guardians and teachers of sound doctrine.

Exhorting in sound doctrine means that the elder is to encourage, comfort, and edify believers. To do this, the elder needs to know sound doctrine, because God's Word and right doctrine encourage, comfort, and edify believers. So an elder must be characterized by doctrinal integrity and the ability to communicate it in various kinds of situations.

It should be noted that the elder must have some ability to teach (1 Tim. 3:3). This does not mean that an elder must be a gifted orator or skilled preacher, but all elders must be able to communicate to others the gospel and sound Scriptural teaching. »

Paul instructs Timothy to: "preach the word; be ready in season and out of season; reprove, rebuke, exhort, with great patience and instruction. For the time will come when they will not endure sound doctrine; but wanting to have their ears tickled, they will accumulate for themselves teachers in accordance to their own desires..." (2 Tim 4:2-3). We need elders sound in doctrine and able to teach it.

Applied to All Christians »

"For though by this time you ought to be teachers, you have need again for someone to teach you the elementary principles of the oracles of God, and you have come to need milk and not solid food." **(Hebrews 5:12)**

"Let the word of Christ richly dwell within you, with all wisdom teaching and admonishing one another with psalms and hymns and spiritual songs, singing with thankfulness in your hearts to God." **(Colossians 3:16)**

Questions » (**1**-No, **2**-Mostly No, **3**-Neutral, **4**-Mostly Yes, **5**-Yes)

1. Do you have a good grasp of a wide variety of biblical doctrines?	
2. Are you willing to speak the truth in love?	
3. Have you at times studied particular doctrines so that you know what you believe from Scripture?	
4. Are you capable of articulating doctrinal themes?	
Enter the total here and on the "Measurement Chart" (page 74)	

REFUTE ERROR | 📖 Word

Summary:
An elder must be able and ready able to identify and refute doctrinal error in all its forms.

Key Verse:
The overseer must be "...able... to refute those who contradict." **(Titus 1:9)**

Description »

The pastoral elder is charged with the positive aspect of teaching, the proclamation of sound doctrine; but he is also charged with the negative aspect of shepherding—refuting error.

This is a qualification that is largely ignored or lost today. The under-shepherds of God's Church are charged with the responsibility of refuting error. This responsibility cannot be shirked or ignored. It must be done.

The Scriptures are clear that the primary weapon that Satan uses against the Church is false teaching (see John 8:44). The elder, out of love and concern for the Church, is to rise up and refute error. Like a shepherd protecting the sheep from the wolves, the elder is to protect the people from false teaching and error (Acts 8:28-29; 1 Tim 1:20).

The rebuking, refuting aspect of shepherding will not win popularity contests. Our cultural sensitivities often stop elders short of actually refuting error; it is not *en vogue* to expose false teaching and error. The elder may pay a toll for offending the beliefs and convictions of those who are led astray. Refuting error is not for the faint of heart but neither is shepherding! But it must be done. Lives are on the line!

The goal of refuting is not to destroy people, but to save them from the consequences of error and false teaching (2 Tim 2:24-26). Elders ultimately want to see people restored, not merely refuted. »

Practically, the pastoral elder needs to have a firm grasp of sound doctrine. He must be a man of the Word. But his knowledge and command of the Word of God must not be passive. He must actively refute error. He must actively expose false doctrine and false living.

Applied to All Christians »

"I am amazed that you are so quickly deserting Him who called you by the grace of Christ, for a different gospel; which is really not another; only there are some who are disturbing you and want to distort the gospel of Christ." **(Galatians 1:6-7)**

"As a result, we are no longer to be children, tossed here and there by waves and carried about by every wind of doctrine, by the trickery of men, by craftiness in deceitful scheming; but speaking the truth in love, we are to grow up in all aspects into Him who is the head, even Christ..."
(Ephesians 4:14-15)

Questions » (**1**-No, **2**-Mostly No, **3**-Neutral, **4**-Mostly Yes, **5**-Yes)

1. Are you able to boldly refute someone who is teaching wrong doctrine?	
2. Are you able to identify false doctrine when it arises?	
3. Can you stand up to false teaching, even if it occurs in someone you respect?	
4. Are you able see and refute the subtle manipulations that false teachers use to gain a following?	
Enter the total here and on the "Measurement Chart" (page 74)	

One-Woman Man |  Family

Summary:
The phrase is best rendered "a one-woman man." An elder has a blameless reputation in his sexual and marital life. He is faithful to his wife and is not flirtatious.

Key Verses:
An overseer must be "...the husband of one wife..." (1 Timothy 3:2)

Appoint elders "...if any man is... the husband of one wife..." (Titus 1:6)

Description »

Some interpret this qualification to be "one wife at a time," but polygamy was not a problem in either the church or society at large in which Paul's original audience lived. Others see this as "one wife in a lifetime," which would exclude a widower who has remarried. It seems hard to imagine how such a situation would affect a man's ability to be an elder. The phrase is best rendered "a one-woman kind of man." Such a rendering is certainly allowable based on the Greek grammar of the phrase, and we would suggest it is the best interpretation of the text. This is a higher standard than just being married. It means an elder is to be above reproach in his sexual and marital life. He is to be blameless in his interaction with the opposite sex. His intimate affection is focused solely and entirely on his wife. He is not flirtatious.

Any compromise in this area of an elder's life brings reproach to the name of Christ, adversely affects his integrity and testimony, and brings confusion and compromise to the local assembly. In this day of moral decay, elders must be proactive in dealing with this important issue.

Among the elders there should be openness about this problem, sensitivity, accountability, and much prayer for protection. A policy delineating an elder's interaction with the opposite sex » can also prove to be a helpful tool. This could include an elder not meeting alone with a woman either in his office or in a home. It could include not traveling alone with a female colleague on a business trip and not traveling alone with a woman in a vehicle.

Even if an elder does not struggle in the area of immorality, he must consider how his interaction with the opposite sex is seen through the eyes of others. He must be wise even in seemingly innocent conversations and physical greetings with women. Compassion and kindness shown by an elder to a woman, if not done carefully, can be misunderstood for something more. "But sexual immorality and all impurity or covetousness must not even be named among you, as is proper among saints" (Eph 5:3).

Applied to All Christians »

"Husbands, love your wives, just as Christ also loved the church and gave Himself up for her, so that He might sanctify her, having cleansed her by the washing of water with the word, that He might present to Himself the church in all her glory, having no spot or wrinkle or any such thing; but that she would be holy and blameless."
(Ephesians 5:25–27; see also Matthew 19:4-9)

Questions » (**1**-No, **2**-Mostly No, **3**-Neutral, **4**-Mostly Yes, **5**-Yes)

1. Do you have a clear view of biblical teaching on divorce and remarriage?	
2. Are you faithful to your wife physically and emotionally? (If single, do you have control of your sexual desires?)	
3. Do women in the church feel comfortable, non-threatened around you?	
4. Are you open and honest about sexual temptation?	
Enter the total here and on the "Measurement Chart" (page 74)	

Summary:
An elder is one whose children obey and respect his leadership in the home.

Key Verses:
An overseer must be ..."one who manages his own household well, keeping his children under control with all dignity..." **(1 Timothy 3:4–5)**

Description »

The crucial assessment when evaluating a man's care for his family is the conduct of his children. To "manage his own household well, with all dignity keeping his children submissive" (1 Tim 3:4) means he guides his children as a concerned, responsible father. He is not a harsh tyrant; he is not a bully.

> **THE QUALIFIED ELDER SHEPHERDS THE SOULS OF HIS CHILDREN.**

The qualified elder shepherds the souls of his children in a respectable and dignified way, caring for their emotional and spiritual needs. He is not simply a disciplinarian who gains obedience by rigid punishment. He models Ephesians 6:4: "Fathers, do not provoke your children to anger, but bring them up in the discipline and instruction of the Lord." He speaks to their hearts within a loving relationship, rather than striving just for appropriate behavior.

The outward fruit of a man's ability to manage his household well is that his children respect and obey his leadership. Titus 1:6 adds that his children are not undisciplined and unruly; they are "not accused of dissipation or rebellion."

When Titus 1:6 speaks of "children who believe," we take this to mean they are "faithful" to the teaching and discipline of the father. This does not mean all the elder's children must be genuine believers, because that is a work of the Holy Spirit. »

But a man's ability to lead and manage the people of God is commensurate with the evidence of having children who are well-behaved.

So managing his household well is about an elder exercising his authority in a way that is dignified, and that results in his household reflecting their regard for his leadership by being under control.

Applied to All Christians »

"Fathers, do not provoke your children to anger, but bring them up in the discipline and instruction of the Lord." **(Ephesians 6:4)**

"But speaking the truth in love, we are to grow up in all aspects into Him who is the head, even Christ..." **(Ephesians 4:14-15)**

Questions » (1-No, 2-Mostly No, 3-Neutral, 4-Mostly Yes, 5-Yes)

1. Are your children consistently well-behaved in public, and do they respect adults?	
2. Do you have a good, healthy relationship with your children, with them respecting you and your words?	
3. Are you successful in not provoking your children to anger?	
4. Do your children speak highly of you and respect you?	
Enter the total here and on the "Measurement Chart" (page 74)	

MANAGES/ HOUSEHOLD

 Personal

Summary:
A man's ability to shepherd his family well is indispensable for managing God's family. This is a proving ground for the quality of his leadership.

Key Verse:
An overseer must be "...one who manages his own household well, keeping his children under control with all dignity (but if a man does not know how to manage his own household, how will he take care of the church of God?)..." **(1 Timothy 3:4-5)**

Description »

An elder's ability to shepherd his own family well is indispensable for managing God's family. This issue is crucial because the home is the proving ground before a man takes on greater responsibility. The church is not a business. The role of elder is not one of boss or CEO. Rather an elder is a gentle fatherly figure who protects, leads, cares for, and feeds the sheep. Those who want to serve as elders will seek to:

"Have this mind among yourselves, which is yours in Christ Jesus, who, though he was in the form of God, did not count equality with God a thing to be grasped, but emptied himself, by taking the form of a servant, being born in the likeness of men. And being found in human form, he humbled himself by becoming obedient to the point of death, even death on a cross" (Phil 2:5-8 ESV).

Like Christ, an elder will not use his position of authority for his own benefit. Rather he will use it for the blessing and benefit of others. An elder is not a religious professional. Rather, he is a servant-leader who lays down his life for the sheep. A man's home life will indicate what sort of shepherd he is.

If a man cannot succeed in managing the few lives of his family members, he will be ill-equipped to manage the larger » extended family of God. He may be a successful businessman and an outstanding leader in the community, yet the true test for eldership occurs behind the closed doors of his home. It is there that his skill and character are revealed. Is he a tyrant? Is he mean-spirited, harsh, controlling, or aloof? Does he act one way in private with his family and another way in public?

An elder must be able to manage his household well.

Applied to All Christians »

"Fathers, do not provoke your children to anger, but bring them up in the discipline and instruction of the Lord." (Ephesians 6:4)

Questions » (1-No, 2-Mostly No, 3-Neutral, 4-Mostly Yes, 5-Yes)

1. Do you enjoy leading your family spiritually?	
2. Do you take the lead in training your children in character?	
3. Is your house tidy, in good state of repair, clean?	
4. Do you maintain a budget of your finances?	
Enter the total here and on the "Measurement Chart" (page 74)	

LOVER OF GOOD |  Personal

Summary:
An elder loves what is good, which dominates his thoughts, establishes his priorities, and motivates his activities.

Key Verses:
The overseer must be "...loving what is good..."
(Titus 1:8)

Description »

A man's heart is revealed by what he loves. Whatever a man loves becomes his passion, the thing to which he ascribes great value, from which he derives great pleasure, and for which he will labor long and hard. Such will dominate his thoughts and motivations and will determine his priorities.

A good man loves what is good (Pr 21:15), while an evil man loves what is evil (Pr 1:22; 2:14; 10:23; 15:21). Implicit in Paul's words is the assumption that the elder loves what is truly good, not just what is represented as "good" by Satan, the flesh, or the world. (We need only recall how Satan deceived Eve regarding what was good.) How, then, can one discern for certain what is truly good? The ultimate standard of "good" is God (Ex 33:19; Matt 19:17), so good must be consistent with His nature. In Philippians 4:8 Paul lists the good things on which our minds should dwell. Micah says it clearly: "He has told you, O man, what is good; and what does the LORD require of you but to do justice, to love kindness, and to walk humbly with your God?" (Micah 6:8).

All Christians are instructed to be devoted to that which is good (Rom 12:9; Phil 4:8), so the elder is to serve as a model for others to follow. Our Lord is the Good Shepherd (Ps 23; John 10:14), and every elder is a good shepherd as he imitates Him in shepherding the flock of God. The elder who loves what is good will lead others to love and pursue what is good, and will seek to turn them from that which is evil.

"Finally, brethren, whatever is true, whatever is honorable, whatever is right, whatever is pure, whatever is lovely, whatever is of good repute, if there is any excellence and if anything worthy of praise, dwell on these things." **(Philippians 4:8)**

Questions » (**1**-No, **2**-Mostly No, **3**-Neutral, **4**-Mostly Yes, **5**-Yes)

1. Are your closest associates godly people?	
2. Do you dwell more on the goodness of God's grace in your life than on your failures and inadequacies?	
3. Do you believe the best about others?	
4. Do you have a hopeful and optimistic view of life, based on the Scriptures?	
Enter the total here and on the "Measurement Chart" (page 75)	

PRUDENT/ SENSIBLE

♥ Personal

Summary:
An elder must be sober-minded, in control of his inner thought life, his emotions, and his attitudes. This must be his overall posture toward himself and others.

Key Verses:
An overseer must be "... prudent..." **(1 Timothy 3:2)**
The overseer must be "...sensible..." **(Titus 1:8)**

Description »

The Greek word *sophron* is translated differently in 1 Timothy 3:2 ("prudent") and Titus 1:8 ("sensible"). To make things a bit more complicated, the word can also be translated "self-controlled," which is the English word used for a different Greek word at the end of Titus 1:8. The translators recognize some overlap in meanings; however, there are differences.

Whereas self-discipline has more to do with the control of specific thoughts and behaviors, being sensible or prudent has to do with an overall posture toward life, that is, not given to excesses or pendulum swings of emotions, behaviors, or perspectives. A prudent elder does not change his mind on a whim nor run after the latest fads. He disciplines his thought life—indeed, his inner life. "For as he thinks within himself, so he is. He says to you, 'Eat and drink!' But his heart is not with you" (Pr 23:7).

The KJV translates the word here as "sober." The elder should be one who does "not ... think more highly of himself than he ought to think; but to think so as to have sound judgment [KJV: soberly], as God has allotted to each a measure of faith" (Rom 12:3). His sober-mindedness models the "living sacrifice, holy and pleasing to God" that should be characteristic of all committed believers who have been "transformed by the renewing of [their] mind" (Rom 12:1-2). »

The prudent elder is in control of his thoughts as they motivate his actions. He is focused on the what, the how, and the when of doing what should be done. This should be characteristic of older men and younger women (Tit 2:2,5). Indeed, it should likewise be the same for elders of the church.

Self-control or self-discipline finds its traction in a man who is sensible or prudent. Yet, conversely, a sensible man who is not self-controlled is useless in living out his Christian walk. Such a man lacks spiritual power and is no use in leading the people of God in holy living.

Applied to All Christians »

"For through the grace given to me I say to everyone among you not to think more highly of himself than he ought to think; but to think so as to have sound judgment, as God has allotted to each a measure of faith." **(Romans 12:3)**

See also the parable of the ten virgins **(Matthew 25:1-13)**, where the Lord Jesus speaks of the importance of prudent behavior.

Questions » (**1**-No, **2**-Mostly No, **3**-Neutral, **4**-Mostly Yes, **5**-Yes)

1. Do you generally display good common sense, particularly in financial areas?	
2. Can you give good counsel on matters dealing with personal relationships?	
3. Do you consistently go to the Word of God when making important decisions?	
4. Are you able to think creatively on how to see the church make progress?	
Enter the total here and on the "Measurement Chart" (page 75)	

SELF-CONTROLLED |  ♥ Personal

Summary:
While self-indulgence characterizes the life of the unbeliever, self-discipline is essential for every Christian, and especially for elders, who set the example for all believers.

Key Verse:
The overseer must be "...self-controlled..." (Titus 1:8)

Description »

The apostle Paul saw self-discipline as a key factor in dealing with the matter of meats offered to idols, as well as his own effectiveness in ministry (1 Cor 8). He also describes self-discipline in athletic terms: "Therefore I run in such a way, as not without aim; I box in such a way, as not beating the air; but I discipline my body and make it my slave, so that, after I have preached to others, I myself will not be disqualified" (1 Cor 9:26-27).

Self-discipline is the exercise of self-control in action in such a way as to avoid what is unprofitable, and to pursue that which is of eternal profit. It is both negative (avoiding the unprofitable) and positive (striving for what is godly and of everlasting good). It is listed as one of the essential steps of Christian maturity in 2 Peter 1:6, to be added to faith, moral excellence, and knowledge.

Why is self-discipline important?
Consider the following reasons:

• Self-indulgence is characteristic of our former way of life as unbelievers (Tit 3:3; Eph 2:1-3), and also of the flesh (Gal 5:19-21).

• Self-indulgence characterizes false teachers (Isa 56:10; Jer 23:1-12; Ezek 34:1-16; 2 Pet 2:1-3). It is also descriptive of the way of life of unbelievers in the end times (2 Tim 3:1-5).

• Lack of self-control makes one vulnerable to Satan's attacks (1 Cor 7:5). »

- Self-control is required of all Christians (2 Pet 1:6) and is a fruit of the Spirit (Gal 5:22-23).
- Self-discipline is necessary for development and exercise of one's spiritual gift (2 Tim 1:6-7).
- Because elders are to lead by example, they must exemplify self-discipline in their own lives.
- Lack of self-discipline disqualifies one (1 Cor 9:27; Tit 1:8) from being an elder.

Applied to All Christians »

"The fruit of the Spirit is... self-control..."
(Galatians 5:23)

"...[supplement] your knowledge [with] self-control..." **(2 Peter 1:6)**

Questions » (**1**-No, **2**-Mostly No, **3**-Neutral, **4**-Mostly Yes, **5**-Yes)

1. Do you usually accomplish tasks on time?	
2. Do you get to meetings on time?	
3. Do you control your tongue?	
4. Do you control your eating?	
Enter the total here and on the "Measurement Chart" (page 75)	

TEMPERATE |  Personal

Summary:
An elder should be temperate, that is, moderate or balanced in his thoughts, behavior, and use of good things—not be given to unwise or self-serving extremes.

Key Verse:
An overseer must be "...temperate." (1 Timothy 3:2)

Description »

An elder should not be given to unwise, self-serving, or self-consuming extremes. The word in 1 Timothy 3:2 is translated "sober-minded" in the ESV, a natural reference to one's use of alcoholic beverages. But, since other qualifications cover that more directly, we best understand this one as more expansive in scope—so the usual translation of "temperate" reflects the broader meaning identified in the lexicons. Interestingly, the KJV renders the word "vigilant," which focuses on the implication of being temperate. An elder ought to moderate his behavior and thinking so that he does not become numb or insensitive to the truth, but remains vigilant.

To be sure, being temperate includes balance in regard to drinking, eating, recreation, clothing, appearance, possessions, sports, toys, use of the media, and conversation. These things in themselves may be good and appropriate in moderation, but when they crowd out one's spiritual sensitivity to life and truth, problems arise. In 1 Timothy 3:11, for example, "temperate" is put in contrast to women who gossip, that is, who get carried away in negative talk about other people, which in turn can render them numb to spiritual needs of the moment. In 1 Thessalonians 5:6, the verb form of the word puts temperance in opposition to being spiritually asleep. A sleeping Christian cannot be temperate or vigilant, for his sleep crowds out his alertness. »

Thus, an elder is "level-headed" in his response to difficult situations, not quickly adopting extreme perspectives. He can evaluate claims to truth or alternative ideas, distinguishing the areas of gray interpretation and application between black and white extremes. He avoids the proverbial "hobby horse," that is, over-emphasizing his own particular point of truth or application of Scripture that puffs him up. Finally, an elder is even-keeled in how he responds to people. This is a temperate man, who remains vigilant to spiritual issues.

Applied to All Christians »

"Older men are to be temperate, dignified, sensible, sound in faith, in love, in perseverance."
(Titus 2:2)

Questions » (**1**-No, **2**-Mostly No, **3**-Neutral, **4**-Mostly Yes, **5**-Yes)

1. Do you regularly deny yourself liberties for the sake of benefiting others?	
2. Can you enjoy the pleasures of life without being dominated by them?	
3. Do you resist the temptation to become overwhelmed by discouraging circumstances?	
4. Are you free from significant and uncontrolled financial debts (not including a house, car, or school loan)?	
Enter the total here and on the "Measurement Chart" (page 75)	

NOT A NEW CONVERT | ♥ Personal

Summary:
An elder must not be a new believer, for he is ill-equipped for the propensity to pride in leaders and the assaults of the devil against them.

Key Verse:
An overseer must be "...not a new convert, so that he will not become conceited and fall into the condemnation incurred by the devil." **(1 Timothy 3:6)**

Description »

Paul's words do not focus on physical age but on the length of time a person has been a believer. The newly planted believer is more susceptible to the temptation of pride than one who is mature in the other character traits of an elder. Pride of leadership is extremely destructive and dysfunctional for the church (see 1 Tim 6:3–5), and so we are unwise to place a new believer in such a position. And we do him no service to expose him in his formative spiritual life to the devil's snare of leadership conceit when he is ill-equipped to handle it. He is less able to "be on guard" for himself, much less the whole church (Acts 20:28). New believers just don't have the experience and knowledge to recognize Satan's seductions and attacks at the outset.

Time is needed to validate one's profession of faith and to demonstrate his character as a growing believer. Note from Titus 1 that the Jewish troublemakers "profess to know God, but they deny Him by their works" (Tit 1:16). Hasty appointment of a new believer bypasses all the character qualifications, for it takes time for the fruits of sanctification to become evident (2 Pet 1:3-11).

When Paul wrote Timothy in Ephesus, the believers were well-taught with elders already in place (Acts 20:17-38). When he wrote Titus, the churches in Crete were young with no existing elders (Tit 1:5). The elders appointed, though new to faith in Christ, would probably be Jews or God-fearing Gentiles, and »

thus would have a good level of godly qualities already
(e.g. "... many of the Jews and of the God-fearing proselytes
followed Paul..." Acts 13:43). While there may be times in
new church planting that newness to faith in Christ might not
prohibit spiritual leadership, the norm should be to avoid placing
new believers into the role of elder.

Applied to All Christians »

"For though by this time you ought to be teachers,
you have need again for someone to teach you
the elementary principles of the oracles of God,
and you have come to need milk and not solid
food. For everyone who partakes only of milk is
not accustomed to the word of righteousness, for
he is an infant. But solid food is for the mature,
who because of practice have their senses trained
to discern good and evil." **(Hebrews 5:12–14)**

Questions » (**1**-No, **2**-Mostly No, **3**-Neutral, **4**-Mostly Yes, **5**-Yes)

1. Have you been a believer for a significant period of time?	
2. Have you faced life experiences involving difficult, trying circumstances and succeeded?	
3. Have you learned how to trust God's promises over time and see them fulfilled?	
4. Have you shown proven character over time in serving in a church ministry?	
Enter the total here and on the "Measurement Chart" (page 75)	

NOT A DRUNKARD  Personal

Summary:
An elder is not controlled by alcohol, does not use it in excess, and is not given to any other substance abuse.

Key Verses:
An overseer must be "...not addicted to wine..."
(1 Timothy 3:3)

The overseer must be "...not addicted to wine..."
(Titus 1:7)

Description »

An elder is not to be a heavy drinker of alcohol. In both passages this qualification is followed by "not pugnacious"/"not violent," obviously alluding to the oft-resulting behavior of over-drinking. Alcohol abuse is a concrete attendant (the means or result of) failure in other qualifications (temperate, self-controlled, lover of what is good, etc.).

The concern is not the beverage or substance itself but its excessive use. Scripture does not preclude an elder from drinking wine but forbids drinking in excess. Jesus at the Canaan wedding endorsed wine as a legitimate beverage by turning water into wine. There is no good proof that wine at the Lord's Supper was anything but alcoholic in nature (although one might argue its relative content). However, elders in particular must "be on guard for [them]selves" (Acts 20:28). Scripture clearly warns of its dangers, so elders must be very careful with its use because of the possible consequences.
"Do not get drunk on wine, which leads to debauchery" (Eph 5:18). Drunkenness is an "act of the sinful nature" (Gal 5:20). "Wine is a mocker and strong drink a brawler; whoever is led astray by them is not wise" (Pr 20:1).

Excessive alcohol affects an elder's sensual perceptions (Pr 23:31-34), clouds his judgment (Pr 31:4), and lowers his moral inhibitions (Hab 2:15, Gen 9:21). In short, alcohol abuse controls the person rather than the person controlling the alcohol. »

Therefore, an elder should not be given to excessive drinking. This would also include not being controlled by other addictive substances like marijuana, sedatives, and pain killers. An elder should be "self-controlled" (Tit 1:8) and Spirit-controlled (Gal 5:18)—which, by the way, are not mutually exclusive. In our day of excessive alcohol use, elders should set the example for the flock of God of moderation, or at times complete abstinence for the sake of weaker Christians.

Applied to All Christians »

"And do not get drunk with wine, for that is dissipation, but be filled with the Spirit..."
(Ephesians 5:18)

"Wine is a mocker, strong drink a brawler, and whoever is intoxicated by it is not wise."
(Proverbs 20:1)

Questions » (1-No, 2-Mostly No, 3-Neutral, 4-Mostly Yes, 5-Yes)

1. Is it true that there are no "consumptive" sins that have mastered you?	
2. Do you make sure no freedom that you enjoy is causing a weaker Christian to stumble?	
3. Are you sober emotionally?	
4. Do you refrain from excessive drinking or taking addictive drugs?	
Enter the total here and on the "Measurement Chart" (page 75)	

NOT GREEDY  ♥ Personal

Summary:
Elders should avoid the love of money because it sets an example of wrong priorities and robs the Lord's people of His shepherding love, care, time and energy.

Key Verses:
An overseer must be "...free from the love of money." (1 Timothy 3:3)

"For the overseer must be ...not fond of sordid gain..." (Titus 1:7)

"Shepherd the flock of God ...according to the will of God; and not for sordid gain..." (1 Peter 5:2)

Description »

This character trait appears in all three elder qualification lists. Titus 1:7 and 1 Peter 5:2 put it as "not fond of sordid gain," and the ESV translates it as "not greedy for gain." The core idea is greed as seen in the unhealthy focus on money. This sin is the root cause of all kinds of evil even today (1 Tim 6:10). In comparing greed with idolatry (Eph 5:5; Col 3:5-6), Paul wants us to have no doubt that greed is like the sin that led Israel astray. It can lead an elder astray from his duty of caring for the people of God. Peter adds that greed is a distinguishable mark of a false teacher (2 Pet 2:2-3).

Greed is the ungodly desire for something more. It sullies the grace of God, screaming He's not been fair with what He has given us. At the heart of the matter, greed is a profound lack of contentment. In fact, the biblical antidote to greed is contentment (1 Tim 6:6, Heb 13:5). We are to flee greed, just as we are to flee idolatry (1 Tim 6:10). Why? Jesus made it clear: "No one can serve two masters, for either he will hate the one and love the other, or he will be devoted to the one and despise the other. You cannot serve God and wealth" (Matt 6:24). »

To be sure, elders must provide for their own needs (1 Thess 3:10) and for their households (1 Tim 5:8). But the more one pursues wealth beyond basic needs, the less one pursues the well-being of God's people. For where our treasure is, there will our hearts (and time and energies) be also (Matt 6:20). Therefore, as elders, we are reminded three times to avoid this sin.

Applied to All Christians »

"For the love of money is a root of all sorts of evil, and some by longing for it have wandered away from the faith and pierced themselves with many griefs." **(1 Timothy 6:10)**

"Make sure that your character is free from the love of money, being content with what you have..." **(Hebrews 13:5)**

Questions » (1-No, 2-Mostly No, 3-Neutral, 4-Mostly Yes, 5-Yes)

1. Do you trust God when tested financially?	
2. Are you generous with your money when people are in need?	
3. Is there evidence that you give generously to the Lord's work in the local church and in missions?	
4. Are your career choice and weekly hours worked influenced by your desire to serve people more than the desire simply to make more money?	
Enter the total here and on the "Measurement Chart" (page 75)	

HOSPITABLE |  Relational

Summary:
Hospitality is characteristic of an elder, who includes others into his life and family circle.

Key Verses:
An overseer must be "hospitable." **(1 Timothy 3:2)**
The overseer must be "hospitable." **(Titus 1:8)**

Description »

Elders are to model what is commanded of all Christians: a sacrificial life that includes hospitality (Rom 12:13). Peter requires it as fervent love for others (1 Pet 4:8-9). Hebrews shows it as a priority even in the midst of persecution (Heb 13:1-2).

The underlying term combines two Greek words meaning "brotherly love" and "stranger." Hospitality is showing brotherly care to those who are not naturally part of one's personal circle of life (3 John 5-6). Mary, Martha, and Lazarus often brought others into their home, most notably the Lord Jesus Christ. Think of the one who lent his room to Jesus and His disciples for the Last Supper and the family of John Mark, in whose home the disciples prayed when James and Peter were imprisoned (Acts 12:12).

The hospitable elder is one who opens his life for others to see him in his own environment. It's a powerful demonstration of humble love and provides connectedness in our digitally impersonal society, providing flesh-and-blood togetherness that encourages depth of sharing. As a spiritual shepherd, hospitality helps you get to know the people better (and conversely). Jesus said, "I know my sheep" (John 10:17). Unrushed and relaxed, hospitality lets people know you care, which may lead to their feeling comfortable approaching you about a need they may have.

Most commonly, hospitality in Scripture meant food and lodging. Elders should be characterized by regularly inviting people into their home for a meal, and if necessary overnight accommodations. But hospitality can also mean taking a » young family to a restaurant, or even meeting someone for coffee to just spend time together. Elders should be characterized as those who invite others into their life. Is it any wonder that heaven is pictured as a banquet?

Applied to All Christians »

"Be devoted to... practicing hospitality."
(Romans 12:10, 13)

"Do not neglect to show hospitality to strangers, for by this some have entertained angels without knowing it." **(Hebrews 13:2)**

Questions » (**1**-No, **2**-Mostly No, **3**-Neutral, **4**-Mostly Yes, **5**-Yes)

1. Do you often use your home to minister to people?	
2. At church meetings, do you go out of your way to meet visitors or people you don't know?	
3. Do you generally have a cheerful countenance?	
4. Do you regularly invite people to church?	
Enter the total here and on the "Measurement Chart" (page 75)	

GENTLE | 👥 Relational

Summary:
Elders must exercise their authority with the gentleness that encourages others, and that invites those in need to approach for help.

Key Verse:
An overseer must be "...gentle..." **(1 Timothy 3:3)**

Description »

Here, Paul employs a Greek word that cannot really be translated consistently with any one English term. We might say it is the sum total of these parts: patience, graciousness, considerateness, kindness, and forgiveness (renderings of the term by various translations). Paul helps us grasp this word in several ways. First, in the same verse he contrasts gentleness with pugnaciousness ("not pugnacious"), and he then links it with being peaceable. Better yet, Paul exemplifies gentleness in his own life and ministry:

"... although we could have imposed our weight as apostles of Christ; instead we became little children among you. Like a nursing mother caring for her own children... As you know, we treated each one of you as a father treats his own children" (1 Thess 2:7, 11 NET).

GENTLENESS IS CHARACTERISTIC OF OUR GOD.

Gentleness is characteristic of our God (Luke 1:78; Tit 3:4), particularly the Lord Jesus (Matt 11:28-30; 12:20; Tit 3:4-5). This is a quality required of all saints (Gal 5:23; Eph 4:31-32; Phil 4:5).

Why is this quality particularly required of elders? Elders have a position of authority in the church, authority over the lives of others. If they are holding fast to the Scriptures, they should also be "right" in their teaching, judgment, and correction. But this authority and "rightness" can easily lead to a harshness and severity. Severity tends to wither tender saints and » inhibit the participation required of all saints. Gentleness conveys approachability, and elders definitely need to portray this quality to those they shepherd. It may well be that it was the gentleness of our Lord Jesus that encouraged sinners to draw near for help. May God grant us His tenderness and gentleness in our care for others.

Applied to All Christians »

"But the fruit of the Spirit is "...gentleness..."
(Galatians 5:22–23)

Questions » (**1**-No, **2**-Mostly No, **3**-Neutral, **4**-Mostly Yes, **5**-Yes)

1. Are you flexible to change your positions on minor issues?	
2. Are you a good and empathetic listener to people?	
3. Are you kind and respectful toward those who are lowly or financially poor?	
4. Are you able to secure the discipline of others without a show of authority?	
5. Are you able to influence others without resorting frequently to a show of power?	
Enter the total here and on the "Measurement Chart" (page 75)	

NOT LORDING |  Relational

Summary:
An elder must not dominate the church like a master who has ultimate authority and power. He must be a servant-leader with all the other qualifications.

Key Verse:
Shepherd the flock of God "...nor yet as lording it over those allotted to your charge..." **(1 Peter 5:3)**

Description »

An elder must not "exercise dominion over" or "domineer" the flock (1 Pet 5:3), in the sense of subduing the congregation to his will. He is not the pinnacle of a leadership hierarchy, with all authority going back to him. The Greek word *katakurieuo* carries an intense form of lordship, using the common root word *kurios* with the prefix *kata*, which can have the notion of "against" or "over" or "down on." It is a harsh, negative word and should never describe an elder.

This is the same word used by Jesus to warn his disciples, "You know that the rulers of the Gentiles lord (*katakurieuosin*, the plural form of the word used in 1 Peter 5:3) it over them, and their great men exercise authority over them. It is not this way among you, but whoever wishes to become great among you shall be your servant, and whoever wishes to be first among you shall be your slave; just as the Son of Man did not come to be served, but to serve, and to give His life a ransom for many" (Matt 20:25–28).

This does not mean that the elders have no authority whatsoever. Paul speaks of elders who rule well (1 Tim 5:17, where the word *prohistemi* means to rule or direct). Furthermore, the congregation should "obey [their] leaders and submit to them, for they keep watch over [their] souls as those who will give an account." But an elder should not covet power and control, » like "Diotrephes, who loves to be first among them..." (3 John 9). He should lead as an act of humble service, like a shepherd who loves his sheep and is willing to give his life for them. If his leadership is characterized by all the other "qualifications," he will truly be a servant-leader.

Applied to All Christians »

"Do nothing from selfishness or empty conceit, but with humility of mind regard one another as more important than yourselves ... Have this attitude in yourselves which was also in Christ Jesus, who, although He existed in the form of God, did not regard equality with God a thing to be grasped, but emptied Himself, taking the form of a bond-servant, and being made in the likeness of men."
(Philippians 2:3-7)

"It is not this way among you, but whoever wishes to become great among you shall be your servant..." **(Matthew 20:26)**

Questions » (**1**-No, **2**-Mostly No, **3**-Neutral, **4**-Mostly Yes, **5**-Yes)

1. Is it true that you do not use manipulation or threats to get your way?	
2. Can you follow someone else's lead without resistance, even when disagreeing?	
3. Do you show a willingness to be a team player?	
4. Do you trust the Lord when others don't follow your lead, and not react in anger or manipulation?	
Enter the total here and on the "Measurement Chart" (page 75)	

NOT QUARRELSOME

 Relational

Summary:
While the elders must wrestle with difficult issues and, at times, challenge and confront wrong, they must not do so in an argumentative and quarrelsome manner.

Key Verse:
An overseer must be "...peaceable (i.e. not quarrelsome)..."
(1 Timothy 3:3)

Description »

The NASB translates the Greek word as "peaceable," but most modern translations render it "not quarrelsome." Paul earlier in the verse set forth the elder qualification of being "not violent" or " not pugnacious." But conflict is more likely to be verbal, and that is why Paul says an elder must not be quarrelsome or argumentative. This means to be predisposed to hostile, unproductive debate, with a desire to "win" the debate and avoid "losing." One's ego has replaced the desire for constructive problem solving and decision making.

There are several reasons why "not quarrelsome" is an important qualification:

• Being argumentative is a manifestation of the flesh, which produces strife and dissension, rather than unity (John 17:23; Gal 5:16-26; Eph 4:3,13).

• Decision making requires the freedom to express opposing views (see Acts 15). Heated debate prompts men to cling even harder to their views and to reply in kind, rather than to listen and come to harmonious decisions (Pr 15:1; 25:15).

• Godly leaders distinguish themselves from false teachers by not being argumentative (2 Tim 2:22-26).

• An elder's confidence must not be in his own debating skills, but rather in the truth of God's Word and the power of His Spirit (Acts 6:4; Phil 3:15). »

• The elder who is not quarrelsome manifests those qualities that testify to the truth and wisdom of their words: "For where jealousy and selfish ambition exist, there is disorder and every evil thing. But the wisdom from above is first pure, then peaceable, gentle, reasonable, full of mercy and good fruits, unwavering, without hypocrisy. And the seed whose fruit is righteousness is sown in peace by those who make peace" (James 3:16–18).

Applied to All Christians »

"But now you also, put them all aside: anger, wrath, malice, slander, and abusive speech from your mouth." (Colossians 3:8)

"This you know, my beloved brethren. But everyone must be quick to hear, slow to speak and slow to anger; for the anger of man does not achieve the righteousness of God." (James 1:19-20)

"It is not this way among you, but whoever wishes to become great among you shall be your servant..." (Matthew 20:26)

Questions » (1-No, 2-Mostly No, 3-Neutral, 4-Mostly Yes, 5-Yes)

1. Do you avoid foolish controversies or arguments about nonessential matters?	
2. Do you promote peace, harmony, and unity when doctrinal issues are discussed?	
3. Can you recognize good points in the views of other people with whom you disagree?	
4. Do you limit discussions and debate before they digress into argumentativeness?	
Enter the total here and on the "Measurement Chart" (page 75)	

Not Quick-Tempered

 Relational

Summary:
An elder, like the God he serves and represents, should not be quick-tempered, but rather slow to anger, predisposed toward grace, compassion, and forgiveness.

Key Verse:
For the overseer must be "...not quick-tempered..."
(Titus 1:7)

Description »

A quick-tempered man is one who is predisposed to anger and easily provoked. His first and natural inclination is toward anger. The NET Bible renders this kind of person "wrathful" in Proverbs 29:22. The NIV puts it this way: "An angry man stirs up dissension, and a hot-tempered one commits many sins." Thus, an angry or wrathful man is also described as hot-tempered.

Being quick-tempered is wrong for anyone, but especially for an elder. "Nothing good, but much evil results from being quick-tempered" (Pr 14:17, 29; 15:18; 25:28; 29:22). If the wise are instructed not even to associate with a man given to anger (Pr 22:24-25), then surely such a man should not be a leader in the church. In fact, godly, wise people are to shun him, which would obviously make it difficult for that angry man to shepherd the people of God.

Further, elders should reflect the character of God, and He is slow to anger: "The LORD is gracious and merciful; slow to anger and great in loving-kindness" (Ps 145:8).

The world is inclined to perceive Christians as angry, hostile people. Elders especially need to reflect the predisposition of our God to be gracious and compassionate, and thus be quick to show grace rather than anger. Wrath may very well be deserved, but it should not be too quick to burst forth. »

His patience toward us should inspire our patience toward others. We are being transformed into conformity with His character (Rom 8:29; 2 Cor 3:18; 2 Pet 1:3-4). The Holy Spirit presently works within us to produce the fruit of the Spirit, which overcomes our fleshly inclination to anger and makes us like Christ (Gal 5:20, 22-24).

Applied to All Christians »

"But now you also, put them all aside: anger, wrath, malice, slander, and abusive speech from your mouth." **(Colossians 3:8)**

"This you know, my beloved brethren. But everyone must be quick to hear, slow to speak and slow to anger…" **(James 1:19)**

"It is not this way among you, but whoever wishes to become great among you shall be your servant…" **(Matthew 20:26)**

Questions » (**1**-No, **2**-Mostly No, **3**-Neutral, **4**-Mostly Yes, **5**-Yes)

1. Do you hold your temper well?	
2. Are you quick to forgive others who have wronged you?	
3. Do you generally rejoice in trials?	
4. Do you generally refrain from correcting your children in anger?	
Enter the total here and on the "Measurement Chart" (page 75)	

NOT SELF-WILLED |  Relational

Summary:
An elder must not be arrogant because it will hinder his relationship with God, make him resistant to grace, and prompt him to use others rather than to serve them.

Key Verse:
The overseer must be "...not self-willed..." (Titus 1:7)

Description »

An elder, Paul tells us, must be "not self-willed" (NASB, NKJV), "arrogant" (ESV, NET), "overbearing" (NIV). Arrogance and self-will are closely related, thus the translation differences. So what is arrogance or self-will? It is an exaggerated, ill-founded self-confidence, a bloated sense of self-importance. Arrogance manifests itself in a blatant disregard for others, including God (1 Tim 1:13; 2 Pet 2:18-20). While humility subordinates self-interest to achieve the well-being of others (Phil. 2:3-8), arrogance casts aside the well-being of others in the pursuit of selfish gain (see Daniel 4, Nebuchadnezzar's pride and fall). While humility embraces God's gracious provisions, arrogance takes credit for the good things that have come our way from the hand of God. Humility acknowledges that God is all-wise and all-powerful; arrogance assumes that one's own wisdom and power are sufficient to bring about what is good.

God's dealings with His people can be summed up in one word: grace. All of Paul's epistles begin with a greeting that includes grace. Arrogance not only resists grace; it despises it: "Why do I need the gracious provisions of God (a kind of divine handout for which I have not worked) when I am fully capable of achieving the same ends by my own wisdom and works?" An elder who has such an attitude cannot convey grace to those he leads, nor can he model the grace of Christ. »

Arrogance is a deadly malady for anyone, so why do the Scriptures specifically speak of it in the midst of elder qualifications? Arrogance is an occupational hazard for every leader (Deut 17:18-20). Jesus made it clear that spiritual leaders must shepherd His flock with a servant's heart, contrasting this with Gentile leaders who "lord it over" their subjects (Matt 20:20-28). Arrogance promotes independence from God; humility promotes dependence on God. Arrogance can neither love God nor one's neighbor. Indeed, it makes God an enemy (1 Pet 5:5).

Applied to All Christians »

"And He went a little beyond them, and fell on His face and prayed, saying, 'My Father, if it is possible, let this cup pass from Me; yet not as I will, but as You will.'" **(Matthew 26:39)**

"Therefore be imitators of God, as beloved children." **(Ephesians 5:1)**

Questions » (**1**-No, **2**-Mostly No, **3**-Neutral, **4**-Mostly Yes, **5**-Yes)

1. Have you surrendered your will to Jesus Christ in all areas of your life?	
2. Is there evidence that at times you have set aside your own will on a decision to support the consensus of the majority?	
3. Do you generally wait on the Holy Spirit's leading before making decisions?	
4. Do you often ask for advice when making decisions?	
Enter the total here and on the "Measurement Chart" (page 75)	

NOT VIOLENT |  Relational

Summary:
In an increasingly violent world, it is vitally important that an elder be characterized by non-violence, thus modeling the character of the Lord Jesus in His earthly ministry.

Key Verses:
An overseer must be "...not... pugnacious..."
(1 Timothy 3:3)

The overseer must be "...not pugnacious, not fond of sordid gain..." (Titus 1:7)

Description »

Paul used a number of different terms to depict the character of an elder in his relationship to others; thus it may be best to take our term literally, to distinguish it from the others. To be "not violent" more literally refers to not "coming to blows." The KJV renders the underlying word as "no striker" and the NASB "not pugnacious" (related to our word "pugilist" for a boxer). Can you imagine an elders' meeting ending with black eyes and bloody noses?

Some cultures have a greater propensity toward physical violence. We do well to remember the violence of some of our OT heroes and the propensity of our Lord's disciples toward use of physical force—"Lord, do You want us to command fire to come down ... and consume them?" (Luke 9:54). Violence is the inclination of our flesh, the use of physical force to get our way (Gal 5:19-21). We might suggest this includes using violent language and threats. Such behavior takes the elder trait of being "not quarrelsome" to an extreme.

How, then, can we discern non-violence in a man? The first place to observe it is in his family life. Paul required that a man must "keep his children under control with all dignity" (1 Tim 3:4). Although this does not forbid corporal punishment, he should not exhibit unrestrained reaction or resort to capricious or » excess punishment, which is child abuse. A man's relationship to his wife should also be considered. He must not be given to the use of physical, emotional, or verbal abuse.

Elders are to demonstrate the saving work of Christ and the transforming power of the Holy Spirit in their lives by evidencing the same non-violence that characterized Jesus and that He required of His followers (Matt 26:52).

....

Applied to All Christians »

"But the fruit of the Spirit is love, joy, peace, patience, kindness, goodness, faithfulness, gentleness, self-control; against such things there is no law." **(Galatians 5:22–23)**

"But I say to you, do not resist an evil person; but whoever slaps you on your right cheek, turn the other to him also." **(Matthew 5:39)**

....

Questions » (**1**-No, **2**-Mostly No, **3**-Neutral, **4**-Mostly Yes, **5**-Yes)

1. Are you able to maintain a concern for others when personally offended by them?	
2. Do you remain calm, not resorting to emotional or physical threats or abuse when wronged by others?	
3. Do your wife and children always feel safe around you?	
4. Do you handle criticism well?	
Enter the total here and on the "Measurement Chart" (page 75)	

MEASUREMENT CHART

Insert the "score" for each qualification from the questions above. Then add up the total at the bottom.

Category	Qualification	Score
Desire	Spirit-Motivated	
	Godly Desire	
	Eager to Serve	
	Not Reluctant	
Integrity	Above Reproach	
	Good Reputation	
	Respectable	
	Devout	
	Upright	
	An Example	
Word	Faithful to the Word	
	Able to Teach	
	Exhort In Sound Doctrine	
	Refute Error	
Family	One-Woman Man	
	Children Behaved	
	Manages Household	

Personal	Lover of Good	
	Prudent/Sensible	
	Self-Controlled	
	Temperate	
	Not a New Convert	
	Not a Drunkard	
	Not Greedy	
Relational	Hospitable	
	Gentle	
	Not Lording	
	Not Quarrelsome	
	Not Quick-Tempered	
	Not Self-Willed	
	Not Violent	

Total

NOTES